Linux

Crash course for newbies

Epris E. Ezekiel

Contents

History

Linux is a prominent open-source operating system. Linus Torvalds founded the project in 1991. Torvalds was a computer science student at the University of Helsinki in Finland when he began working on the Linux project as a personal project. The name Linux is a combination of his first name, Linus, and Unix, the operating system that influenced his work. At the time, most operating systems were proprietary and costly. Torvalds wanted to develop an operating system that was freely available to anyone who wanted to use it, thus he initially distributed Linux as free software under the GNU General Public License. This allowed anyone to use, alter, and redistribute his source code.

Early versions of Linux were primarily used by technology enthusiasts and software developers, but it has since expanded in popularity and is

1

now used in a wide range of devices, including servers, smartphones, and embedded systems. Linux is widely used in servers, supercomputers, and enterprise environments and is regarded as one of the most stable, secure, and trustworthy operating systems available.

Today, Linux is one of the most commonly used operating systems in the world, accounting for an estimated 2.76% of all desktop computers and more than 90% of the world's top supercomputers, as well as around 71.85% of all mobile devices that run Android, which is, you guessed it, Linux-based. The Linux community has grown to encompass thousands of developers and users who contribute to the design and maintenance of the operating system.

Chapter 1

What is Linux?

Linux is a strong and adaptable set of operating systems that are free to use and distribute. Linus Torvalds created it in 1991. What's cool is that anyone can examine how the system works because the source code is freely available for exploration and modification. This openness enables individuals from all around the world to collaborate and make Linux even better. Since its inception, Linux has evolved into a robust and secure operating system used in a variety of applications, including laptops, cell phones, and large supercomputers.

It is noted for its efficiency, which means it can complete a large number of jobs fast, as well as its cost-effectiveness, which means it is inexpensive to operate. Many individuals enjoy

Linux, and they are part of a large community that shares ideas and helps one another. As technology advances, Linux will continue to evolve and remain significant in the world of computing.

What is the Linux Operating System?

The Linux Operating System is a sort of operating system that is comparable to Unix and is based on the Linux kernel. The Linux Kernel functions as the operating system's brain, managing how the machine interacts with its hardware and resources. It ensures that everything runs smoothly and efficiently. However, the Linux Kernel alone does not constitute a complete operating system.

To produce a fully functional system, the Linux Kernel is paired with a collection of software applications and tools known as Linux distributions. These distributions prepare the Linux Operating System so that users can run apps and complete tasks on their computers securely and efficiently. Linux distributions exist in a variety of flavors, each built to meet the unique needs and tastes of users.

How is Linux different from other operating systems?

Linux is similar to other operating systems you've used in the past, such as Windows, macOS (previously OS X), and iOS. Linux, like other operating systems, includes a graphical interface and the software you're used to, such as word processors, photo editors, and video editors. In many circumstances, a software developer may have created a Linux version of a program you already use on other systems. In a nutshell, Linux is accessible to everybody who can use a computer or other electronic device.

But Linux differs from other operating systems in several fundamental ways. First and possibly most crucially, Linux is open-source software. The code used to construct Linux is free and open to the public to examine, change, and contribute to, provided they have the necessary expertise.

Linux is also unique in that, while the essential components of the Linux operating system are generally the same, there are numerous Linux variants with varying software selections. This means that Linux is extremely adaptable, as it is not limited to apps like word processors and web browsers. Linux users can also select essential components, such as how the system displays graphics and other user interface elements.

What can you accomplish with Linux? Linux may serve as the foundation for almost any IT project, including containers, cloud-native applications, and security. It lies at the heart of some of the world's most important sectors and enterprises, from knowledge-sharing websites like Wikipedia to the New York Stock Exchange to mobile devices running Android (a specific-use distribution of the Linux kernel with additional software). Linux has evolved to become the de facto standard for operating highly available, dependable, and essential workloads in data centers and cloud deployments.

It includes a variety of use cases, distributions, target systems and devices, and capabilities, all tailored to your specific requirements and workloads. By 2027, all SAP clients will have transitioned to SAP HANA, an in-memory relational database management system that operates exclusively on Linux.

Microsoft has embraced Linux and open source in various ways, such as developing an SQL Server for Linux and open-sourcing its framework (.NET Core/Mono) so that it can operate on any platform, allowing Linux developers to create apps utilizing that framework.

Chapter 2

Who uses Linux?

You probably already use Linux, whether you realize it or not. According to several user surveys, servers running Linux create between one- and two-thirds of all web pages on the Internet.

corporations and individuals pick Linux for their servers because it is secure and adaptable, and you can get excellent support from a big user community, as well as corporations like Canonical, SUSE, and Red Hat, which all provide commercial support.

Many of the gadgets you own, including Android phones and tablets, Chromebooks, digital storage devices, personal video recorders, cameras, wearables, and more, run Linux. Under the hood, your car runs Linux. Even Microsoft Windows includes Linux components as part of the Windows Subsystem for Linux (WSL).

Linux Distribution

Linux distribution is an operating system that consists of a collection of software based on the Linux kernel, or distribution, which includes the Linux kernel as well as supporting libraries and software. You may get a Linux-based operating system by downloading one of the Linux distributions, which are available for a variety of devices such as embedded devices and personal PCs. There are over 600+ Linux distributions available, and some of the most popular ones include:

- ✓ Deepin
- ✓ OpenSUSE
- ✓ Fedora
- ✓ Solus
- ✓ Debian
- ✓ Ubuntu

- ✓ Elementary
- ✓ Linux Mint
- ✓ Manjaro
- ✓ MX Linux

The architecture of Linux.

The Linux architecture includes the following components:

- ➤ **System utility:** The Linux Operating System provides system utilities, which are key tools and programs for managing and configuring many parts of the system. These utilities perform a variety of activities, including software installation, network configuration, system performance monitoring, user and permission management, and much more. System utilities simplify system administration operations, allowing users to more efficiently maintain their Linux systems.

- **Hardware Layer:** The hardware layer contains all of the computer's physical components, including RAM (Random Access Memory), HDD (Hard Disk Drive), CPU (Central Processing Unit), and input/output devices. This layer interacts with the Linux operating system and provides the resources required for the system and programs to function effectively. The Linux kernel and system libraries provide communication and control of these hardware components, ensuring that they work together seamlessly.

- **Shell:** The Shell is the Linux Operating System's user interface. It allows users to interact with the system by typing commands that the shell interprets and executes. The shell acts as a liaison between the user and the kernel, routing the user's requests to the kernel for processing. It enables users to accomplish a variety of functions, including application execution, file management, and system configuration.

➢ **System library:** Linux uses system libraries, often known as shared libraries, to implement the operating system's numerous capabilities. These libraries include pre-written code that apps can use to complete specific tasks. Developers can save time and effort by adopting these libraries, which eliminate the need to write the same code repeatedly. System libraries serve as an interface between applications and the kernel, offering a consistent and efficient means for applications to communicate with the underlying system.

➢ **Kernel:** The kernel is the foundation of the Linux-based operating system. It virtualizes the computer's common hardware resources, giving each process its virtual resources. This creates the illusion that the process is the only one executing on the machine. The kernel is also responsible for preventing and resolving disputes between processes. There are various sorts of kernels:

- ✓ Microkernels
- ✓ Exo kernels
- ✓ Hybrid kernels
- ✓ Monolithic Kernel

Advantages of Linux

- ✓ It completes all duties successfully despite having limited hard disk space.
- ✓ It is quick and simple to install via the web. It can also be installed on any hardware, including your old computer system.
- ✓ Linux is compatible with a wide range of file formats.

- ✓ Linux provides a high level of flexibility. There is no need to install the entire Linux suite; you can install only the necessary components.
- ✓ It is network-friendly.
- ✓ Linux outperforms other operating systems. It permits a large number of individuals to work simultaneously and efficiently.
- ✓ It maintains the user's privacy.
- ✓ It gives excellent stability. It rarely slows down or freezes, and it does not require a reboot after a short period.
- ✓ It enjoys widespread community backing.
- ✓ Linux is freely available for usage on the internet.
- ✓ There are several Linux distributions available, so you can choose one based on your needs or preferences.
- ✓ Linux allows for easy and frequent software updates.

- ✓ This does not imply that Linux is completely secure; it does have some malware, but it is less vulnerable than any other operating system. Therefore, no anti-virus software is required.
- ✓ In terms of security, Linux is the most secure operating system.
- ✓ The primary advantage of Linux is that it is an open-source operating system. This means that the source code is freely available to everyone, and you can contribute, edit, and distribute it to anybody without restriction.

The disadvantages of Linux

- ✓ It isn't particularly user-friendly. As a result, newbies may find it complicated.
- ✓ Unlike Windows, it has fewer peripheral hardware drivers.

Chapter 3

Events That Lead to the Creation of Linux

The origin of Linux, one of the world's most popular open-source operating systems, can be traced back to numerous significant events and the efforts of a few individuals. The following is a list of the important events that contributed to the creation of Linux.

> ➤ **Linux in the Consumer Market:** Linux has also made its way into the consumer market, with mobile devices, smart TVs, and other consumer goods all running on the platform.

> ➤ **Linux in Enterprise:** With the emergence of cloud computing and the Internet of Things, Linux has gained traction in the industry. Linux is currently commonly used as an operating system on

servers, mainframes, and supercomputers. It's also utilized in embedded systems, mobile devices, and the Internet of Things.

➢ **Linux Distribution Growth:** As Linux gained popularity, various groups of developers began to create their own versions of the operating system, known as distributions. Some of the most popular distributions include Red Hat, Debian, and Ubuntu. These distributions include the Linux kernel as well as a variety of his packages of user-friendly tools and software, making it simple for both developers and end users to utilize his Linux.

➢ **Enterprise Adoption:** In the late 1990s and early 2000s, Linux's open-source nature made it more versatile, cost-effective, and safe than proprietary operating systems like Windows, making it a popular choice for corporations and businesses. Companies began hiring people. As Linux's popularity grew, commercial support and services for it emerged.

- ➢ **Linux community growth:** In the years that followed, Linux soon became popular among programmers and enthusiasts. A developer community grew around Linux, with members producing code, filing bug reports, and providing comments to help the operating system evolve.

- ➢ **Release of Linux 0.01:** Linus released his initial Linux version, Linux 0.01, in September 1991. It was a command-line operating system that was freely available via the Internet.

- ➢ **Linux was born:** Linus Torvalds, a 21-year-old student, began developing a new operating system known as Linux in 1991. Linus was motivated by his Minix, and he utilized its source code as the foundation for his initiatives. He also relied extensively on Unix design concepts.

➤ **Minix was born:** In the early 1980s, Andrew S. Tanenbaum, a computer science professor, developed Minix, a compact Unix-like operating system. Minix was created as an educational tool, with the source code made available to students.

➤ **Unix development:** In the late 1960s and early 1970s, Bell Labs developed the Unix operating system, which strongly impacted Linux. Unix was created as a multi-user, multi-tasking operating system that has found widespread usage in science and research.

Chapter 4

How to Get Started with Linux

Are you new to Linux and unsure how to get started? It's simpler than you might imagine. Whether you're coming from macOS or Windows, or are simply curious about Linux, this beginner's guide to using Linux will provide you with valuable information.

Step 1: Selecting a Linux distro

How do you utilize Linux? First, select a Linux distribution, typically abbreviated as "distro." A distribution is a unique operating system based on the Linux kernel. The number of distros available is enormous and rising, so how should you choose?

That depends on your gear and computing habits. Is your PC old or has a low-end processor? Choose a distribution that claims itself as lightweight or resource-friendly. Are you a multi-media content creator? Prepare for a heavier, studio-focused distribution.

If you're a new Linux user looking for something simple and familiar, Linux Mint, Manjaro Linux, or Elementary OS are all good options. Whatever distribution you choose, make sure your hardware fulfills the specifications.

To get a feel for any of them before committing, you can run a distro inside your browser or on a virtual computer.

Is Linux free?

At this point, you might be wondering: Is Linux truly free?

The answer is yes. They are enterprise editions that are not intended for the average user. Some Linux developers may ask for a donation or offer to sell you a pre-written image CD, but downloading and using the distribution is free.

What is a Desktop Environment (DE)?
Many distributions will come with different desktop environments (DEs) or "flavors." Simply described, a DE is a certain type of desktop appearance and structure. To get a preview, search for photographs of a specific DE online.

Unsure which DE to choose? Linux aficionados will have strong ideas about the "best" DE, but a new user should not think too hard about it; simply choose the one that sounds most appealing to you, and if you have problems with it, switching to another is simple.

Step   2:   Create   a   Bootable   Drive
After   selecting   a   distribution,   you   must
download the ISO file from the distro's website.
The ISO contains the distribution's basic files
and architecture, and you must copy it to a USB
stick or SD card before you can boot the Linux
"image" on your device.

Don't   be   intimidated   if   something   seems
complicated. There   are   many   image   writing
programs available that will accomplish the task
for you with a few clicks. This instruction covers
how to write the Ubuntu ISO to a drive, and the
process is similar for the majority of popular
Linux distributions. If necessary, you can burn
the contents of an ISO file to a DVD, which will
boot and install your distribution. However, it is
an outdated and unreliable method that is not
recommended.

Step 3: Test a Linux Distribution

With a boot disk in hand, you can start the "live" version of your distribution. A live boot will illustrate the functionality of the distribution on your device without requiring any adjustments.

Connect the boot disk to your computer while it is powered off, then turn it on. Your computer should immediately locate and boot the live CD. It isn't as complicated as it sounds.

How to Change Your PC's Boot Order to Boot From USB

Once you've completed a successful live session,

feel free to experiment with apps, connect to the internet, and play music and videos. If you experience problems during the live boot, such as no sound or a fuzzy screen, it could be a hint that the distribution isn't for you. Many problems in Linux are fixable, but others require a significant amount of effort, which is not a good way to begin your Linux journey.

Step 4: Install Linux

The installation process varies slightly between distributions.

It normally entails reformatting your hard drive, selecting a region, and a keyboard layout, and performing installation and upgrades.

Important: If you have any important files saved on your device, make a backup before attempting a Linux installation. A full overwrite will wipe any existing data, and while a dual boot configuration is feasible, the potential of inadvertent data erasure remains.

In a live boot session, there will usually be a link in the welcome screen or desktop to start the installation. When you click the install link, an on-screen instruction will direct you through the entire process.

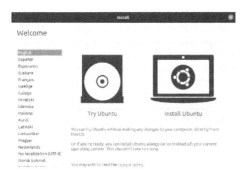

Installation will always take time, so please be patient, even if your screen appears frozen. However, having another PC or smartphone on hand is useful in case you encounter any problems.

Step 5: Connect to the Internet on Linux

Connecting to the internet in Linux works similarly to other operating systems. A network management tool will often appear in your taskbar, and when launched, it will display a list of available Wi-Fi networks.

If Wi-Fi does not appear to work, you may need to download additional drivers for your wireless network card. Connect with an Ethernet cable instead, or switch to a different device and search the internet for a solution for your unique equipment.

Don't forget that all popular distributions have

active communities accessible via forums, social media, and chat apps. Knowledgeable individuals ready to help you with your Linux difficulties will always be there, so visit your distro's website and look for community links.

Step 6: Launching Apps in Linux
How does one run an application in Linux? Your distribution will most likely include an app-launching widget akin to the original Windows start menu or macOS Launchpad.

Instead of utilizing a graphical user interface (GUI) tool, you can easily run apps via the command line interface (CLI), often known as the terminal.

Find your distro's terminal emulator (Ctrl+Alt+T will usually launch it), then type a launch command and press Enter.

To start the Firefox browser, enter the following command into your terminal:

```
firefox
```

Step 7: Downloading Software for Linux Most distributions' basic installations will contain at least your fundamental PC utilities and accessories, such as the firewall, network manager, notepad, and an internet browser. But what if you need additional apps or a specific app that you're used to utilizing on other platforms?

Many distributions include a software browsing program that provides an experience similar to the Apple program Store or the Microsoft Store. Look for something called Software Manager or AppCenter, where you may find and install popular apps like Firefox, Spotify, and Steam.

If you don't see a certain software listed, the app's website will usually include a link or instructions for downloading the Linux version. Some applications, such as Microsoft Office, do not have an official Linux version. There are methods around this, however.

Step 8: Customize Your Linux Experience

This is where Linux shines: Windows and macOS have limited customization options, whereas practically everything on a Linux desktop can be modified with the correct tools and know-how. You can even make your Linux desktop appear like Windows or macOS.

You should find some options in your distro's appearance settings menu, but you may go even further by searching for instructions unique to your DE.

Chapter 5

How to Install Linux

A step-by-step guide for installing Linux on a USB flash drive.

Are you wondering how to install Linux? If you want to switch from your existing operating system or just have more options, this article will walk you through the Linux installation procedure step by step.

Installing "Linux" is a bit misleading. When people say this, they mean installing a distribution (distro) that employs the Linux kernel (an operating system's core) as a foundation for a full-fledged operating system. Popular distributions include Ubuntu, Fedora, and Debian.

If you're new to Linux, as with any new system, you may need some time to get to know it. However, distros like Ubuntu ensure that Linux is easy to use and does not differ significantly from Windows or macOS.

To help you get started, we'll go over how to install Linux. We'll teach you how to install Linux (using the popular Ubuntu distro) using a USB ISO drive, which you can also generate on a Windows PC.

There are multiple ways to install Linux. For all of them, we'll boot from a USB flash drive, which is a simple solution. You'll only need a machine with a USB port and a USB flash drive with at least 16GB of storage.

Caution: We have used well-known and reliable third-party software (such as bootloaders and distros). The instructions in this post can be applied to different software, but be sure you're downloading from a trusted source.

Before we begin the installation process, we need to transfer our Linux distribution to a USB flash drive. There are various ways to install Linux, such as downloading installation files from the Internet. However, network installations require a reliable and fast internet connection; otherwise, the installation process may fail.

Installing Linux via a USB flash drive is quick and simple; therefore, we chose that approach here.

❖ **Download the UNetbootin executable file (do not run it).**

To run Linux from a USB, you'll need third-party software that creates a bootable drive. There are various bootloaders to pick from, but for this instruction, we've gone with UNetbootin, which is simple to download and install.

Download the executable file from unetbootin.github.io, but do not execute it yet because we will need to obtain an ISO image before we can install it. Save the.exe file where you can find it.

❖ **Download the Ubuntu disk image (ISO).**

You'll need an ISO image of the distribution you intend to use. We're using Ubuntu, a popular Linux distribution for laptops and desktops. This is known as a Desktop in Ubuntu, but it can also be referred to as a disk image (as we will see in the following step), a desktop image, or an ISO.

Download the Ubuntu disk image at
ubuntu.com/download.

❖ **Install the bootloader.**

Insert the USB stick into the computer. Then launch the UNetbootin (or another bootloader) executable file. This opens a pop-up window with numerous fields to fill out before you can proceed.

DiskImage

You have the option of selecting a Distribution from a selection list or uploading a DiskImage (which we downloaded from Ubuntu previously). Select DiskImage and navigate to the ISO file you saved in Step 2. If you pick Distribution, make sure you choose the most recent version of the software from the list.

Type

You should ensure that a USB Drive is selected.

Drive

Make sure you point this to the drive that your USB is currently utilizing. Before moving on to the next stage, double-check that it is not pointing to another external drive, as the bootloader procedure may overwrite data.

When you're ready, click OK.

❖ **Wait for the bootloader installation to complete.**

The installation process will now start. The bootloader software needs to download, extract, and copy files before installing the bootloader, which can take some time. When you receive the indication indicating the installation is complete, select Exit.

Your Linux distribution is now on your USB flash device.

Chapter 6

Differences between Linux and Windows

Linux

Linux could be a free and open-source operating system that adheres to established operating system standards. It provides a programming interface as well as programs that are compatible with operating system-based platforms and offers a wide range of applications. A UNIX operating system also includes various independently developed components, resulting in a UNIX operating system that is completely interoperable and free of proprietary code.

Windows

Windows may be a commissioned operating system in which ASCII text files are inaccessible.

It is intended for people who do not have programming knowledge, as well as business and other industrial users. It's basic to use. The difference between Linux and Windows packages is that Linux is fully free of charge, whereas Windows is a commercial program that is pricey. An associate operating system could be a program designed to control the PC or computer hardware. An associate acts as a bridge between the user and the hardware. Linux is an open-source program that allows users to view ASCII text files, perhaps improving the system's code victimization. In contrast, users cannot read ASCII text files in Windows, even though it is an authorized operating system. Let's look at the differences between Linux and Windows:

Linux	Windows
Linux is an open-source operating system.	While Windows is not an open-source operating system.
Linux is free of charge.	Although it is pricey.
The file name is case-sensitive.	While the file name is case insensitive.
Linux uses a monolithic kernel.	This uses a hybrid kernel.
The hybrid kernel is utilized here.	While windows are inefficient.
A forward slash is used to separate the directories.	While the backslash is used to separate folders.

Linux provides higher security than Windows.	Linux provides higher security than Windows.
Linux is commonly utilized in hacking-related systems.	While Windows is not particularly efficient for hacking.
There are three sorts of user accounts – (1) Regular, (2) Root, and (3) Service account.	There are four sorts of user accounts. (1) Administrator, (2) Standard. (3) Child; (4) Guest
Linux file naming convention is case-sensitive. Thus, sample and SAMPLE are two distinct files in the	In Windows, you cannot have two files with the same name in the same directory.

Linux/Unix operating system.	
The root user is the superuser, with full administrative powers.	The administrator user has full administrative access to machines.

Conclusion

Linus Torvalds' 1991 development of Linux has resulted in considerable advances. It began as a simple operating system for personal computers and has since grown into a popular and recognized platform that powers everything from supercomputers to smartphones. Because Linux is an open-source operating system, a large and active developer community has been able to contribute to its development and maintenance, resulting in a highly adaptive and dependable operating system. It is popular among both consumers and businesses because of its low cost and versatility. Linux remains a major participant in the world of technology, and its impact may be felt in a variety of different fields.